Enid Blyton's

·BIBLE·STORIES·

SAMSON, THE STRONG GIANT
& GIDEON, THE BRAVE SOLDIER

OLD TESTAMENT
BOOK 9

GRANADA PUBLISHING

SAMSON, THE STRONG GIANT

Once there lived a man so big and strong that people called him a giant. His name was Samson, and he was one of the Children of Israel.

He was a strange man to look at, very tall and broad, and his hair fell all round his shoulders, for he had never had it cut. He was so strong that he could kill lions with his bare hands.

The Israelites, Samson's people, had a great enemy in those days, called the Philistines. It was Samson's joy and delight to annoy the Philistines, and spoil their harvests.

Once he sent wild foxes down into the valley, with lighted torches tied to their tails. The torches set fire to the ripe corn, and to the vineyards, and burnt them all up. These fields belonged to the Philistines, and they were very angry when they saw that Samson had caused them to be burnt.

"We will march against the Israelites and fight them," said the Philistines. "We will tell them

that we must have Samson as our prisoner."

So, to the great fear of the Israelites, the Philistines marched into their land to fight them. "We have come to get Samson," they said.

Then three thousand of the Israelites went into the hills to seek for Samson. They found him and told him why they had come. "Our land will be over-run with the enemy unless we take you to the Philistines," they said.

Samson let them bind him fast with new cords, and then he was taken to the Philistines. But just as he reached them, he snapped the ropes, picked up a big bone lying nearby and rushed at the astonished Philistines. He killed a thousand of them with the bone, and others fled away in terror.

Many more marvellous deeds the giant did, and the Philistines grew to be very much afraid of him. Always they hoped to get him into their power, and punish him for all he had done to them.

Now Samson loved one of the Philistine women called Delilah. When the Philistine chiefs heard this they went to Delilah, and made a plan with her.

"You must find out why Samson is so strong, so that we may perhaps rob him of his great strength," they said. "We will pay you well, if you do this."

So Delilah promised, for she wanted money. The next time that Samson came to see her, she praised his great strength, and said, "Can anything make you as weak as other men?"

Samson laughed. He was fond of making jokes, and he joked with Delilah. "If I am bound with seven green sticks that have never been dried, I am as weak as other men," he said.

Delilah told the Philistines this and they were

full of joy. Now they knew how to rob Samson
of his giant-like strength. So the next time he
came to see her, Delilah had ready seven
green sticks, which bent easily. She bound his

wrists with them, laughing. Samson laughed too.

When he was asleep, Delilah called out loudly as a signal to the hidden Philistines, "Samson, Samson, the Philistines are upon you!"

The giant leapt up and broke his bonds at once, running out of the house and escaping before the Philistines could catch him.

Twice more Delilah asked Samson how he could be made weak, and each time he joked, and told her untrue things. She believed him, and then was angry when she found he had been telling her lies.

"You do not love me or you would tell me truly," said Delilah, weeping. She grumbled at him, and wept for many days and at last Samson told her the truth.

"Well, I will tell you what you want to know," he said. "It is a simple thing. As long as I have hair on my head then I am strong. If it were shaved away, then I should be as weak as other men."

When Samson fell asleep, Delilah sent for a man to cut off Samson's hair and to shave his head. And then when she called out "Samson, Samson, the Philistines are upon you!" he could not escape. All his great strength was gone, and he was as weak as other men.

The Philistines fell on him and bound him. They gave him a terrible punishment, for they blinded him so that his eyes could no longer see. They put him into prison, bound with heavy chains, and made him grind corn. There was poor Samson, a blind and unhappy man.

But when his hair began to grow he felt his great strength returning to him, and he waited for a day to come when he might use it against the men he hated.

One day the Philistines gave a feast. "We will

send for Samson, and make him show us his strength," they said. "He is a blind giant now, and he cannot do anything against us."

So they sent for the blind man, and they laughed at him, and made him do many things he did not wish to do. When the sport was over Samson spoke to the boy who led him.

"Take me to the pillars upon which this house is built," he said. "I would lean on them to rest myself."

The boy took him to the great stone pillars. On them rested the enormous flat roof of the house. Many people were on the roof, watching Samson, and many more were below it.

Then Samson took hold of the two middle pillars, which held up the house, and he dragged at them with all his might. They broke in half, and the house fell with a terrible noise, killing hundreds upon hundreds of the Philistines.

Samson died with them, a blind and miserable giant. So strong a man was he that his tale is still told, and men still wonder at his mighty strength.

GIDEON, THE BRAVE SOLDIER

T here was once a young man called Gideon. He was one of the Children of Israel, who had settled in a fair land, and had made it their home. They tilled the ground and kept fine flocks and herds.

Gideon's home had once been down on the plain, where golden corn waved, but now he had to live in a cave up on the hillside. Enemies had come and reaped the harvest that Gideon and his people had sown, and had stolen away many of their sheep and cattle too.

Gideon remembered the day when he had seen the Midianites, the enemy, coming in their thousands. The Midianite chiefs were princes, richly dressed, owning many camels and having thousands of men under them. They came riding up in the distance, and Gideon and the Israelites watched them in fear.

"Here are the Midianites! They come to steal our harvest!" cried the Israelites. Quickly they fetched what weapons they had and made ready to fight.

The Midianites set up their black tents. It was

plain that they meant to stay. They fought the Israelites and drove them up into the hills. They took their fine harvest, and stole their flocks and herds.

"Now this is a punishment to us!" said Gideon. "We have forgotten our true God, who led us out of Egypt, where we were slaves. We pray now to wooden idols, we do not pray to the true God. We are justly punished!"

The Israelites had to live in caves and dens whilst their enemies lived in the valley below. If they had any grain to thresh, they had to do it secretly, or the Midianites would come to take it.

Gideon had a little grain. He went to a big wine-trough made out of rocks in the hills, stood in it, and began to thresh his corn there. He was well hidden.

He was working hard when he heard a voice.

"The Lord is with you, mighty man of valour!"

Gideon looked out of the trough, and saw a stranger sitting under a tree.

"Sir," said Gideon, "if the Lord is with us, why have we been driven from our fields by the enemy?"

"You shall save your people from the Midianites," said the stranger, and this surprised Gideon very much.

"How shall I do that?" said the young man. "Am I not the least in my father's house?"

"I will be with you," said the stranger, and then Gideon felt afraid, for surely no one would say such things to him unless he were God or his angel.

"Wait a while," said Gideon. "I will fetch you food." He brought out some meat and bread and broth, and put them on a nearby rock.

The angel touched them with his staff, and

fire came up out of the rock and the food
vanished. Then the angel was gone, and
Gideon was alone on the hillside.

Gideon wondered very much about all that
the angel had said. The Midianites went when
winter came, and the Israelites crept down from

the hills to till their fields once more, hoping
that their enemy would not come back.

But alas, the Midianites once again put their
black tents in the valley when the harvest was
ready, and the Israelites had to flee to the

hills, leaving their corn to be reaped again by the enemy.

Then Gideon made up his mind that the time had come for him to do as the angel had said. He blew a trumpet and sent messengers to tell the young men of Israel to come to him and fight against the enemy.

Twenty-two thousand young men came, and Gideon was proud of his great army. But God did not need so many. He spoke to Gideon.

"Tell your young men that all those who are afraid may go home." Then Gideon told them, and so many went home that he had only ten thousand left.

"There are still too many," said God. "Take your men down to the water, and watch them as they drink. Some will go down on their knees and drink from the river. Some will take water into their hands and lap it. Put aside all those who lap from their hands, for those are the men I will use."

Gideon watched the men drinking. Only three hundred lapped from their hands, a small

army but big enough for God.

Then the Lord put a strange plan into Gideon's mind, and Gideon went to tell his men.

"To-night we conquer the Midianites," said Gideon. "I will tell you God's plan. First, you must divide into three companies."

This was done. Then Gideon gave each man three things – a trumpet, an empty jar, and a torch.

"Put your lighted torch inside your jar," he said, "then the enemy will not see its light too soon. now, you must all do as I do. Follow me to the camp of the enemy."

It was night-time. The men, their lighted torches hidden in their jars, followed Gideon. He went to the camp of the enemy and surrounded it.

Then, quite suddenly, Gideon raised his

trumpet, blew it loudly, and shouted, "The sword of the Lord and of Gideon!" He broke his jar, and the light of his torch flashed out at once.

Then all the other men did the same. They blew their trumpets, smashed their jars, waved their lighted torches and shouted loudly, "The sword of the Lord and of Gideon! The sword of the Lord and of Gideon!"

The Midianites awoke in terror. They saw the lights all round the camp, they heard the trumpets and the shouting. "A great army has come upon us!" they said, and they rushed out into the darkness to fight. They struck each other, for they were taken by surprise, and did not know which was enemy and which was friend.

Soon the whole of the Midianite army was running away, and Gideon and his men chased them, shouting fiercely.

When the people knew that Gideon and his
three hundred men had conquered the great
hosts of the enemy, they praised Gideon, and
wanted him for their king.

But Gideon would not be king. He shook his

head when the messengers came to beg him to rule over his people.

"I will not be your king and rule over you," he said. "Only God shall be your ruler. Give thanks to him."

·THE·END·